KNOW
THEGAME

The FA
LEARNING

Soccer

Produced in collaboration with
the Football Association

A&
C B

Produced for A & C Black by

Monkey Puzzle Media Ltd
Gissings Farm, Fressingfield
Suffolk IP21 5SH

Published in 2006 by

A & C Black Publishers Ltd
38 Soho Square, London W1D 3HB
www.acblack.com

Fifth edition 2006

ISBN-10: 0 7136 7700 7
ISBN-13: 978 0 7136 7700 3

A CIP record for this book is available from the
British Library.

Note: While every effort has been made to ensure
that the content of this book is as technically accurate
and as sound as possible, neither the author nor the
publisher can accept responsibility for any injury or
loss sustained as a result of the use of this material.

A & C Black uses paper produced with elemental
chlorine-free pulp, harvested from managed
sustainable forests.

Acknowledgements
Thanks to the following at the FA: Ian Blanchard
(Head of National Referee Development) and
Jonathan Wilson (Marketing Manager, FA Learning).
Cover and inside design by James Winrow for
Monkey Puzzle Media Ltd
The publishers would like to thank Umbro (pages
4, 5 right and 6) and Mitre (page 7 top) for their
photographic contributions to this book.
All other photographs courtesy of Empics.
Illustrations by Dave Saunders

KNOW THE GAME is a registered trademark.

Printed and bound in China by C&C Offset Printing Co., Ltd.

Note: Throughout the book players and officials are
referred to as 'he'. This should, of course, be taken to
mean 'he or she' where appropriate.

CONTENTS

04 THE GAME
04 Equipment
06 The ball

08 FIELD OF PLAY
08 Pitch care
08 Pitch markings
12 Goal area
13 Corner flagposts

14 MATCH DURATION AND SCORING
14 Start and restart of play
15 Time added on
16 Suspension of play
16 Substitutions
17 Scoring a goal
18 Finding a winner

20 BALL IN AND OUT OF PLAY
20 Throw-in
22 Goal kick
22 Corner kick

24 OFFENCES
24 Direct free kick offences
24 Indirect free kick offences
28 Misconduct
31 Goalkeepers

32 OFFSIDE
34 Offside in action

38 FREE KICKS

40 PENALTY KICKS
42 Penalty kick questions

44 CONTROLLING THE GAME
44 Referee
46 The referee's duties
48 Assistant referee
50 The fourth official
50 Diagonal system of control

52 MODIFICATIONS
52 School soccer
52 Modifications for others
53 Mini soccer

54 THE FOOTBALL ASSOCIATION
54 Becoming a referee

56 GLOSSARY

60 FOOTBALL CHRONOLOGY

62 INDEX

THE GAME

Soccer is an exciting game for two teams of up to 11 players a side. One member of each team must be a goalkeeper. Each team tries to attack to score goals and defend to stop goals being scored against them. The team who has scored the most goals at the end of the game is the winner.

EQUIPMENT

Players' kit

A footballer usually wears:

- a jersey or shirt
- shorts
- socks
- footwear
- shinguards.

A player should not wear anything that could cause injury to another player or himself. He may wear spectacles at his own risk if the referee, the official in charge of a match, chooses to allow them.

Clothing colours

The colours of the two teams' clothing, known as their strip, should be distinguishable from each other and from the referee. Goalkeepers have to be clearly seen and they wear different colours to the outfield players and the referee. Some leagues insist on players wearing numbers on the backs of their shirts.

Visible underwear such as cycling shorts is allowed, but only if it does not extend past the top of the knee. It must also be of the same colour as the main colour of the player's shorts.

 Goalkeepers usually wear padded gloves, which help grip the ball.

> **Keep your socks covering your shinguards at all times.**

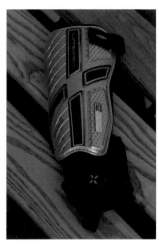

Frank Lampard displays good forward vision while running with the ball.

Modern shinguards have an elastic loop (bottom) to fit under the sole of your foot.

Putting it right

The referee can ask a player to leave the field if an item of the player's kit breaks any laws.

If the ball is in play (see page 14), then the referee will instruct the player to leave the pitch when it next goes out of play. The player must wait until the referee has re-inspected him and is happy that the kit is in order. He can then come back onto the pitch the next time the ball is out of play.

SHINGUARDS

Shinguards can be made of rubber, plastic or a similar material. There are no rules on their size but they must help protect a player's shins (the front of their leg below the knee).

Footwear

Footwear is a crucial part of a player's kit. Much research has gone into producing lightweight boots and shoes which are comfortable, provide the right amount of grip for the playing surface and enable players to feel the ball on their foot. Footwear still has to conform to regulations. It is the player's responsibility to make sure that his footwear is not dangerous to another player.

A white waterproofed ball is easier to see on winter days.

Soccer boots come in many designs. Some have studs, pimples or blade shapes moulded into their soles for grip on different types of pitches. Others come with interchangeable studs.

THE BALL

The leather balls used in the distant past could soak up water and become heavy. Today, many balls come with a waterproofed surface which keeps water out. This means that the ball doesn't increase in weight even in wet conditions. No part of the way a ball has been made should pose a danger to players.

THE BALL MUST:

- be completely round (spherical)
- have a casing of leather or another approved material
- measure 68–70cm (27–28 in) in circumference
- weigh 410–450g (14–16 oz) at the start of the game
- be inflated to a pressure of 0.6–1.1 atm, which equals 600–1100g/sq cm (8.5–15.6 lb/sq in) at sea level.

Different sizes

The ball used in the adult game is a size 5. A size 3 or 4 is usually recommended for primary and lower-secondary school children. For games played by school children on artificial pitches, balls with protected seams are available.

 The size-5 ball approved and used in the English Premier League.

The ball can only be changed during the game with the consent of the referee.

Steven Gerrard and Sol Campbell battle it out during England training.

FIELD OF PLAY

The Laws of the Game allow the pitch, known as field of play, to vary in size but it must always be longer than it is wide. The markings within the pitch (see diagram) are fixed and must remain constant. Clubs should try to obtain a pitch which is as close to the length and width of pitches used in international matches.

PITCH CARE

A good quality pitch is in every club and all players' interests. A level field of grass which drains water well needs to be regularly cared for, closely mown and divots replaced.

All-weather pitches

In places where drainage is a problem or the pitch is in use every day, some clubs and authorities lay down an artificial 'all-weather' surface instead of grass turf.

PITCH MARKINGS

Touchlines

Goal lines, touchlines and the halfway line are all known as boundary lines. They are part of the field of play. Touchlines are the longest boundary lines. When the ball passes completely over them it is out of play. Play is then restarted with a throw-in (see page 20).

Here are the measurements for the pitch and all its markings.

The corner area

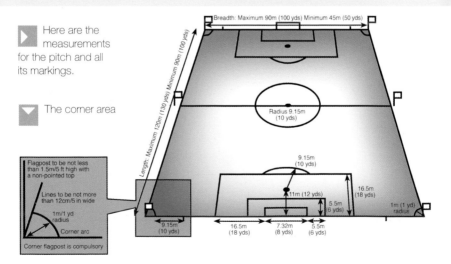

Breadth: Maximum 90m (100 yds) Minimum 45m (50 yds)

Length: Maximum 120m (130 yds) Minimum 90m (100 yds)

Radius 9.15m (10 yds)

9.15m (10 yds)

11m (12 yds)

16.5m (18 yds)

5.5m (6 yds)

1m (1 yd) radius

9.15m (10 yds)

16.5m (18 yds)

7.32m (8 yds)

5.5m (6 yds)

Flagpost to be not less than 1.5m/5 ft high with a non-pointed top

Lines to be not more than 12cm/5 in wide

1m/1 yd radius

Corner arc

Corner flagpost is compulsory

Halfway line

This line divides the field into two equal halves. A player cannot be offside if he is in his own half at the moment the ball is played.

Goal lines

Goal lines are the lines at each end of the field, joining and at right angles to the touchlines. The width of a goal line must match the thickness of the goalposts and the crossbar. When the whole of the ball passes over the goal line on the ground or in the air, the ball is out of play. The game is restarted in one of three ways:

> **PITCH DIMENSIONS FOR INTERNATIONAL MATCHES**
>
> Maximum 110 x 75m
> (120 x 80 yds)
>
> Minimum 100 x 64m
> (110 x 70 yds)

- a goal kick (when the ball has last been played by or touched an attacking player)

- a corner kick (when the ball has last been played by or touched a defending player)

- a kick-off after a goal has been scored (when the ball passes between the goal posts and under the crossbar).

> **At kick-off, you must stay in your own half until a player has kicked the ball.**

These are the names of all the pitch markings on the field of play.

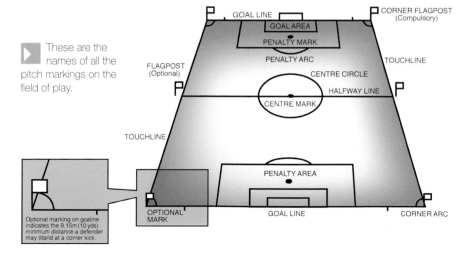

GOAL LINE • CORNER FLAGPOST (Compulsory) • GOAL AREA • PENALTY MARK • PENALTY ARC • FLAGPOST (Optional) • CENTRE CIRCLE • TOUCHLINE • HALFWAY LINE • CENTRE MARK • TOUCHLINE • PENALTY AREA • OPTIONAL MARK • GOAL LINE • CORNER ARC

Optional marking on goaline indicates the 9.15m (10 yds) minimum distance a defender may stand at a corner kick.

Centre circle

The centre circle has a radius of 9.15m (10 yds) and the centre spot is from where kick-offs are taken. The centre circle cannot be entered by an opposition player until the kick-off has been taken.

Penalty area

Measuring 40.3 wide x 16.5m deep (44 x 18 yds), the penalty area serves a number of important functions. It indicates or shows:

- the area of the field of play in which a penalty is awarded if a defending player commits one of the ten 'direct free kick' offences (see page 24)

- where on the pitch the ball may be handled by the defending goalkeeper

- the area beyond which the ball must be kicked for it to be in play from a goal kick or a free kick taken by a defending side in its own penalty area

- the area outside which all players except the goalkeeper and penalty taker must stand when a penalty is taken

- the area outside which all opposition players must remain whilst a goal kick or free kick is taken by a defending side.

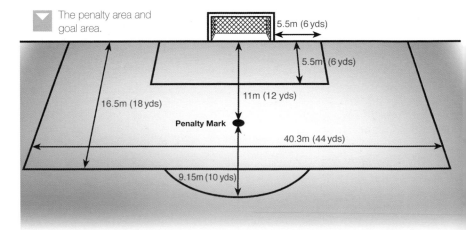

The penalty area and goal area.

5.5m (6 yds)

5.5m (6 yds)

11m (12 yds)

16.5m (18 yds)

Penalty Mark

40.3m (44 yds)

9.15m (10 yds)

Penalty mark

The penalty mark is 11m (12 yds) from the centre of the goal line. The ball must be placed on the mark when a penalty is taken.

Penalty arc

Although not part of the penalty area, the penalty arc is used when a penalty is taken. Players from both teams must not encroach into the area defined by the arc until the penalty taker has kicked the ball.

Technical area

At most grounds, there are technical areas around the team benches. These may extend 1m to the side of the dugout and must stop at least 1m from the touchline. Managers, coaches and other team officials can get off their bench to give instructions to their team. However, they must stay inside the technical area and return to the bench afterwards.

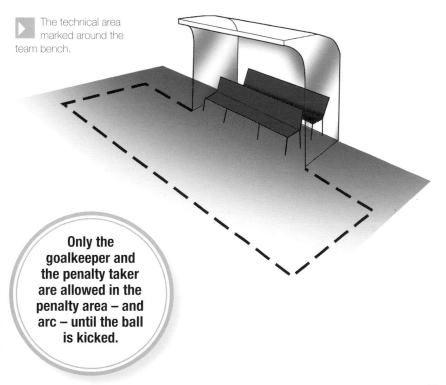

The technical area marked around the team bench.

Only the goalkeeper and the penalty taker are allowed in the penalty area – and arc – until the ball is kicked.

GOAL AREA

The goal area is the area in which the ball must be placed for a goal kick. Although most goalkeepers place the ball in the most forward corners of the goal area, the ball can be placed in any part of the goal area.

Goals

The posts and crossbar can be square, rectangular, round or elliptical. Whatever their shape, they must not measure more than 12cm (5 in) wide or deep. The goalposts and the crossbar may only be made of wood or metal. They must be white.

Goal Mouth

The goal mouth measures 7.32m (8 yds) between the inside of the two goalposts. It should also measure 2.44m (8 ft) from the ground to the lower edge of the crossbar.

Goal Nets

Nets are only compulsory in certain competitions, but their use is advised. They should be properly pegged down and fastened to the back of the goalposts and bars. This stops them being a hazard to the goalkeeper. Neither wire mesh for netting nor any kind of advertising on the goals, corner flags or field of play is allowed.

> **Consider placing the ball further into the goal area for your kick. This might give you better footing as you kick the ball.**

The goal, shown securely fitted with a goal net.

2.44m (8 ft)

7.32m (8 yds)

CORNER FLAGPOSTS

Corner flagposts mark the corners, and help the officials in deciding whether a ball passing close to the corner has gone over the touchline or the goal line. They must be:

- not less than 1.5m (5 ft) high

- not be pointed at their top

- firmly fixed but not too stiff and rigid or they could cause injury if a player collides with them.

HALFWAY FLAGS

Halfway flagposts are not essential. If they are used they must be opposite the halfway line and at least 1m (1 yd) outside of the touchline.

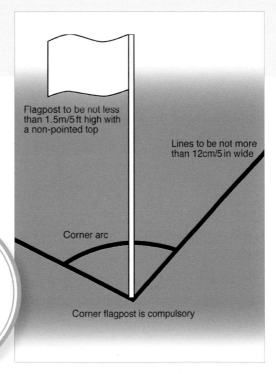

The corner flag and corner arc pitch marking.

Flagpost to be not less than 1.5m/5 ft high with a non-pointed top

Lines to be not more than 12cm/5 in wide

Corner arc

Corner flagpost is compulsory

Corner flags cannot be removed or bent away from their upright position to help a player taking a corner kick.

MATCH DURATION AND SCORING

The match is divided into two equal periods, known as halves. Each normally lasts 45 minutes, unless competition rules allow it to be shorter. In between is a half-time period, which cannot last longer than 15 minutes and must be stated in the competition's rules. It cannot be altered without the referee's agreement.

START AND RESTART OF PLAY

The captains of both teams usually shake hands with each other and the referee and then a coin is tossed and one captain calls. Whoever wins can choose which end their side defends in the first half. The other side kicks off the first half.

After half-time, ends are changed and the game is restarted by the team that did not kick off the first half. A kick-off also restarts the game after a goal is scored. The team who let the goal in take the kick-off.

The Kick-Off

At the kick-off and until the ball is in play:

- both sets of players must remain in their own half

- the opposing team's players must stay at least 9.15m (10 yds) from the ball

- the ball must be placed so that it is still and on the centre mark.

When the referee signals, a player can kick off. The ball must be kicked forward into the opponent's half and once it has been kicked and moved it is in play.

STRAIGHT FROM KICK-OFF

A goal can be scored direct from a kick-off. In 1995, Damien Mori of Adelaide City, Australia scored a goal straight from a kick-off, which (according to FIFA) was timed at just 3.67 seconds.

Once not twice

The kicker must not play the ball a second time until it has been touched by another player. If he does, and the game has otherwise correctly started, an indirect free kick is awarded to the opposing side. Any other infringement concerning the start of play sees the kick-off retaken.

TIME ADDED ON

In all games a referee has the power to make allowances in either half of the game for time lost through substitution, removal from the field of injured players, time wasting or any other cause. He must extend time to allow a penalty kick to be taken.

In certain competitions, the rules allow for periods of extra time and their duration. When extra time is necessary, the captains again toss for choice of end. The interval between the end of normal playing time and the start of extra time is up to the referee.

Alan Shearer, Scott Parker and Michael Chopra of Newcastle discuss tactics before restarting the game.

SUSPENSION OF PLAY

If play is stopped for an infringement of the laws, the game is restarted by a free kick. Play can also be suspended:

- because of injury to a player or official

- when the ball becomes lodged between two players and the situation may cause injury

- when interference from outside the game, such as by a spectator, causes the game to be stopped

- when the ball bursts.

If the ball was passed out of play just before the suspension, the game is restarted by the correct method such as a throw-in or goal kick.

Drop Ball

If the ball was in play as the suspension occurs, the referee performs a drop ball. The referee drops the ball between opposing players who can only touch it once it reaches the ground. If they touch it before, the drop ball is performed again.

SUBSTITUTIONS

In most league and cup competitions, up to three substitutions can be made from a bench featuring between five and seven substitutes. Each competition has its own exact rules but in all cases, the names of the substitutes must be given to the referee. In friendly matches, up to six substitutions per team are allowed.

During a stoppage in play, any player may be replaced, providing the referee is informed. Referees have to caution players who:

- leave the field of play without permission, unless in the normal course of the game such as running over the touchline to take a throw-in

- enter or re-enter the field of play after the game has started without the referee's permission.

CHANGING THE GOALKEEPER

Any of the other players may change place with the goalkeeper provided that:

- the referee is informed before the change is made
- the change is made during a stoppage in the game.

SCORING A GOAL

For a goal to be scored, the whole of the ball must pass over the whole of the goal line, between the posts and under the crossbar. The ball must not be thrown, carried or moved by the hand or arm of an attacker. If a defending player handles the ball and it passes over the line into the goal, a goal is scored.

Should a goal be prevented by a defending player (other than the goalkeeper) handling the ball, the player is shown a red card and sent off. If the handball occurred in the penalty area, a penalty is awarded. If it occurred outside of the penalty area, a direct free kick is awarded.

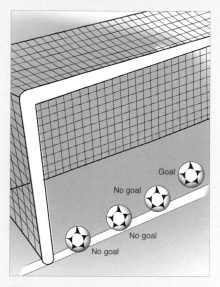

The whole of the ball must be completely over the goal line for a goal to be scored.

David Beckham watches from the bench, after being taken off during a 2005 England match against Colombia.

Goals from free kicks

A goal cannot be scored from an indirect free kick (see page 24) unless the ball has touched another player from either side before it passes into the goal. If, when taking an indirect free kick, a player kicks directly into his opponents' goal, a goal kick is awarded to the defending team.

If a defender taking either type of free kick from outside his penalty area kicks into his own goal, a corner kick is awarded to the attacking team.

FINDING A WINNER

Some competitions need a winning team from a match to win the final or progress to the next round. There are three common methods used to determine a winner of a game when the game is tied after normal time:

- away goals – if the match is over two legs, the team with the most away goals wins

- extra time – this usually consists of two periods of 15 minutes

- penalty shootout.

Jerzy Dudek saves Andriy Shevchenco's penalty in the 2005 UEFA Champions League final. The save helped Liverpool to beat AC Milan.

Penalty shootouts

These are sometimes used instead of extra time or if extra time or the Golden Goal does not determine a winner.

1) The referee decides which goal to use and the captains toss a coin, with the winning team choosing whether to go first or second.

2) The teams take kicks in turn for up to five kicks each until a winner is determined.

3) If the scores are level after five kicks each, the teams continue each taking one kick in turn until a winner is determined after an equal number of kicks.

▼ Proof that goalkeepers take crucial penalties – Ricardo of Portugal taking the winning penalty in the Euro 2004 quarter-final against England.

Unlike a regular penalty, the taker in a shootout can only kick the ball once and cannot follow up a rebound.

TAKING THEIR TURN

Each player can only take one kick in a shootout until everyone has had a turn including the goalkeeper. Some shootouts continue so long that players may have to take a second penalty.

BALL IN AND OUT OF PLAY

The ball is out of play when it has wholly crossed the goal or touchline in the air or on the ground. If the ball goes out of play but swerves back to land in the field of play, it has still gone out of play. The position of the ball and not the player matters. For instance, the player controlling the ball can be out of play, but providing the ball remains in play, the game continues.

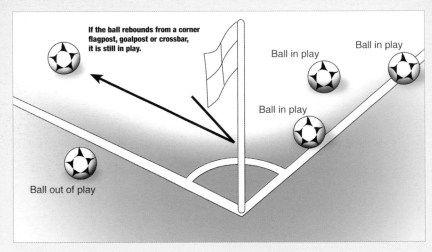

If the ball rebounds from a corner flagpost, goalpost or crossbar, it is still in play.

Ball in play

Ball in play

Ball in play

Ball out of play

The ball has to wholly cross the goal line or touchline to be out of play.

You cannot be offside receiving the ball directly from a throw-in.

THROW-IN

A throw-in is taken from where the ball first completely crossed the touchline. It is awarded to the team who did not last touch the ball before it went out of play. If a throw is taken improperly (commonly called a foul throw), the throw-in is retaken by the opposing team.

All opponents must stand at least two metres from the point at which the throw-in is taken.

Taking a throw-in

The thrower must deliver the ball from behind and over his head. The thrower's arms should then move continuously forward to the point where the ball is released. This can be a little ahead of the body of the player – it does not have to be whilst the thrower's hands are directly over his head. A throw-in must be:

- taken from the position where the ball passed over the touchline

- made with both hands throwing the ball

- made by the thrower facing the pitch as the ball is delivered

- made with part of both of the thrower's feet on the ground and on or outside of the touchline.

AFTER THE THROW-IN

Once the ball crosses the line from a legal throw-in, it is in play. The thrower aims to get back on the pitch immediately. But he cannot play the ball until it is touched by another player from either team. If he does, the opposition team are awarded a free kick.

 Phil Neville takes a throw-in for Everton.

You cannot score a goal direct from a throw-in. Nor can a goalkeeper collect a thrown-in ball with his hands.

GOAL KICK

If the ball was last touched by the attacking side and goes wholly over the defending side's goal line but not into the goal, a goal kick is awarded. It can be taken from any point inside the goal area but must travel outside of the penalty area. If not, it is retaken.

Opposition players must stay outside of the penalty area until the ball leaves it. The goal kick taker can be the goalkeeper or an outfield player. He must not kick the ball a second time before it has been touched by another player. If he does, an indirect free kick is awarded.

A goal can be scored direct from a goal kick but only against the opposing team.

Special circumstances

There are two special circumstances regarding free kicks awarded in the goal area. These free kicks are taken:

- from anywhere inside the goal area if it is awarded to the defending team
- from a point on the front goal area line nearest to where the offence occurred, if an indirect free kick is awarded to the attacking team.

Dropped ball

If play is suspended when the ball is inside the goal area, a dropped ball takes place on the front goal area line. It occurs nearest to where the ball was as play was stopped.

CORNER KICK

A corner kick is awarded when the whole of the ball is last touched by a defending player and completely crosses the goal line. A member of the attacking team takes the corner, placing the ball inside the corner quadrant (see diagram). A goal may be scored direct from a corner kick but an own goal cannot.

Opponents must stay at least 9.15m (10 yds) from the corner until the ball is in play. The corner taker cannot play the ball a second time until another player has touched it. If he does, an indirect free kick is awarded.

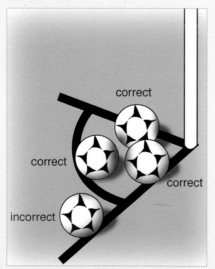

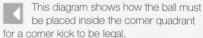

This diagram shows how the ball must be placed inside the corner quadrant for a corner kick to be legal.

Goal kicks and corners should be taken with as little delay as possible.

Chris Kirkland takes a goal kick.

OFFENCES

There are a number of offences that the referee must keep a lookout for – these are all designed to protect the safety of the players and to ensure that the game is played in good spirit. Committing an offence will result in a free kick and the player may be punished with a caution or, in some cases, a sending off.

DIRECT FREE KICK OFFENCES

A direct free kick will be awarded to the opposition side if a player commits any of the following offences:

- spits at an opponent

- holds an opponent

- when tackling an opponent, makes contact with the opponent before the ball

- handles the ball deliberately (except the goalkeeper handling in his own penalty area).

A direct free kick is also awarded if a player commits any of the following offences in a manner considered by the referee to be careless, reckless or using excessive force:

- charges an opponent

- pushes an opponent

- strikes or attempts to strike an opponent

- kicks or attempts to kick an opponent

- trips or attempts to trip an opponent

- jumps at an opponent.

If any one of the ten offences above is committed inside the player's own penalty area, then a penalty kick is awarded.

INDIRECT FREE KICK OFFENCES

Some offences are penalised by the award of an indirect free kick against the offending side. These offences are:

- dangerous play (such as attempting to kick the ball near the head of another player)

- impeding or obstructing the progress of an opponent when not playing the ball

- preventing the goalkeeper from releasing the ball from his hands

- committing any other offence not mentioned in Law 12 for which play is stopped to caution or dismiss a player.

Goalkeeping offences

An indirect free kick is awarded if a goalkeeper, inside his own penalty area, commits any of the following offences:

- takes more than six seconds while controlling the ball with his hands, before releasing it

- touches the ball again with his hands after it has been released and has not touched any other player

- touches the ball with his hands after it has been deliberately kicked to him by a teammate

- touches the ball with his hands after he has received it directly from a throw-in taken by a teammate.

See page 31 for more on goalkeepers.

Kicking an opponent

Striking or attempting to strike an opponent

An example of dangerous play. It is up to the referee to decide if the actions of a player could be dangerous to others.

Handling

A player 'handles the ball' if he has deliberately carried, struck or blocked the ball with his hand or arm. Sometimes, it is impossible for the player to get his hand or arm out of the way before a ball strikes it. The referee must decide if the handball was deliberate and, if not, should let play continue.

Tripping

Tripping is not limited to the use of feet and legs to unbalance an opponent or make them fall. Some players try to throw their opponents by stooping low in front or behind of them. Simulating a trip – pretending that an opponent tripped you – is unsporting behaviour and should earn a caution from the referee.

Pushing and holding

Players use their arms for balance and protection but they must never hold back an opponent or push him away from the ball. This can occur when players' arms become interlocked. Players must not hold an opponent's shirt or shorts and if the referee judges it to be unsporting behaviour will caution the player as well as awarding a free kick against him.

Jumping at an opponent

Jumping at an opponent includes jumping into a tackle with both feet and is penalised by the referee. Jumping for the ball is allowed providing it does not, in the referee's opinion, endanger an opponent.

 Charging an opponent

 Tripping, using the legs

Unfair impeding

A player playing or attempting to play the ball is allowed to shield or screen the ball. He can do this by putting his body between the ball and his opponent but must not push or hold him. A player is not allowed to stop or slow the progress of an opponent by blocking his path when he is not attempting to play the ball. This is known as unfairly impeding.

Even if you are being unfairly obstructed or held, you may not use your hands to push away an opponent.

Shirt holding is not allowed and will result in a free kick.

Pushing an opponent

The player in blue is unfairly impeding the progress of the player in red by blocking his path.

MISCONDUCT

All spectators enjoy seeing fair and skilful play, not spoiled by the use of unfair or dishonest tactics. Unfortunately, some players chose to act or react in unsporting ways and it is the referee's duty to punish players for misconduct.

The referee must caution a player and show a yellow card if he:

- enters or re-enters the field of play without the referee's permission

- deliberately leaves the field of play without the referee's permission

- persistently infringes the laws of the game

- delays the restart of play

- fails to respect the required distance when play is restarted with a corner kick or free kick

- shows dissent (unwillingness to accept the referee's decision) by word or action

- is guilty of unsporting behaviour.

The referee will show a red card and send the player from the field of play, if:

- is guilty of violent conduct or serious foul play (see below)

- uses offensive or insulting or abusive language and/or gestures

- denies the opposing team a goal or an obvious goal-scoring opportunity by deliberately handling the ball (does not apply to goalkeeper in his own penalty area)

- denies an obvious goal-scoring opportunity by an offence punishable by a free kick or penalty kick

- spits at anyone

- receives a second caution in the same match.

Violent conduct and serious foul play

This occurs when a player is violent or very aggressive towards an opponent when not challenging for the ball. It also occurs if a player attacks anybody else such as a teammate, an official, manager or a spectator. Serious foul play is the use of unnecessary or excessive force in unfairly challenging an opponent for the ball.

Never argue with a referee or show dissent by gestures or words. Remember, the referee's decision is final.

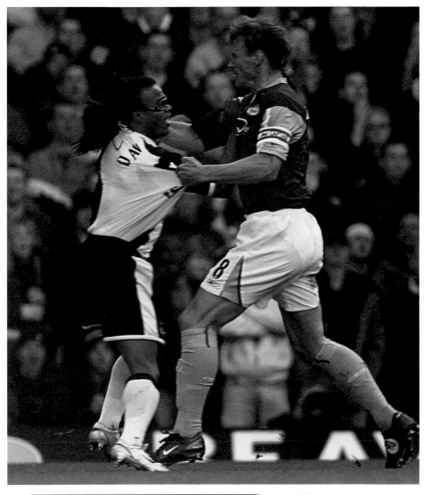

Edgar Davids and Teddy Sheringham get to grips in the Premiership.

SENDINGS OFF

A player can be dismissed, sent off for a single straight red card or by accumulating two yellow cards in the same game. If a player has been sent off, he cannot sit in the technical area and must leave the area around the field of play.

GOALKEEPERS

A goalkeeper can play the ball with his head, body and feet like any other player but inside his own penalty area, he can also handle the ball. Goalkeepers are subject to other special rules which they must be aware of.

The goalkeeper is considered to be in control of the ball when:

- touching it with any part of his hands or arms

- deliberately parrying the ball with his hands or arms.

The goalkeeper is not considered to be in control of the ball when, in the referee's opinion, the ball rebounds accidentally from the goalkeeper after he has made a save.

In the area

If a goalkeeper comes out of the penalty area and dives to handle the ball, part of his body may be on the ground outside the area. Providing that the ball remains in the penalty area whilst it is handled by the keeper, this is not an offence.

The six-second rule

With the ball in his possession, the goalkeeper must not waste time. He has a maximum of 6 seconds to hold the ball before releasing it into play. He can take as many steps as he likes within his penalty area during this time.

The backpass rule

Goalkeepers now need to take great care when the ball is deliberately kicked to them by a teammate or thrown directly from a throw-in. A keeper must not handle the ball in this situation otherwise an indirect free kick will be awarded to the opposition team. The free kick will be taken from where the keeper first handled the ball; it is not an offence for the outfield player to pass back to the goalkeeper.

Paul Robinson makes a dramatic stop on Didier Drogba's shot.

DEALING WITH A BACKPASS

Don't risk handling a ball kicked back to you by a teammate. Clear the ball with your foot or, if it is a high ball, your head or body.

OFFSIDE

A player is in an offside position if he is nearer the defending team's goal line than both the ball and the next-to-last opponent. He can be level with the next-to-last opponent but not closer to goal. The two opponents do not have to be the goalkeeper and a defender. They can be two outfield players.

If the ball is passed forwards whilst someone is in an offside position, the referee usually stops play. The assistant referee helps spot offside infringements and signals using his flag to alert the referee.

It is not an offence in itself for a player to be in an offside position and the referee can choose to not stop play but to let it continue if the player is offside but:

- is not in active play or interfering with an opponent

- is not gaining an advantage for his team, the attacking side, by being offside.

The assistant referee holds out his flag to show that there has been an offside.

Time your attacking runs forward to stay onside until the ball is ahead of you.

A player must be 'onside' (i.e. not offside) at the moment when the ball is played and passed forwards. If the attacker runs offside after the ball has been passed ahead of him, that is not an offence. There are a number of other situations where a player is not offside and should not be penalised:

- if he is in his own half of the pitch
- if he is level with the last-but-one defender
- if the player is level with at least two opponents.

Players also cannot be offside if they receive the ball:

- directly from a throw-in
- directly from a corner kick or goal kick.

AFTER AN OFFSIDE

If the referee stops play for an offside decision, the defending team gets an indirect free kick. It is taken from the place where the offside player was when the infringement happened.

Zinedine Zidane of France is caught offside by the Croatian defence (who are keenly signalling to the assistant referee what has happened).

OFFSIDE IN ACTION

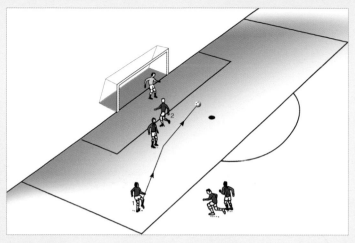

Example 1

As attacker **1** plays the ball across the penalty area, attacker **2** is both in front of the ball and in front of the next-to-last opponent. Attacker **2** is in an offside position and in an active area of play. The assistant referee should signal as soon as attacker **1** plays the ball that attacker **2** is offside.

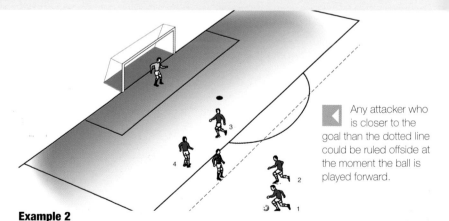

Any attacker who is closer to the goal than the dotted line could be ruled offside at the moment the ball is played forward.

Example 2

Attackers **2**, **3** and **4** are all ahead of the ball. Attacker **2**, though, has two opponents between him and the goal line so is not offside. Attackers **3** and **4** only have one opponent between them and the goal line. If attacker **1** plays the ball towards them, then they are in offside positions.

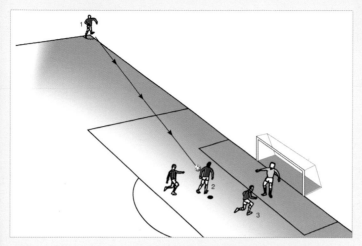

Example 3

Attackers **2** and **3** cannot be offside if they receive the ball direct from a corner kick. If, however, the ball goes direct from the corner kick to attacker **2** who then plays it to attacker **3**, then he, attacker **3**, will be penalised for being offside. In the same way, you cannot be offside if you receive the ball directly from a throw-in or a goal kick.

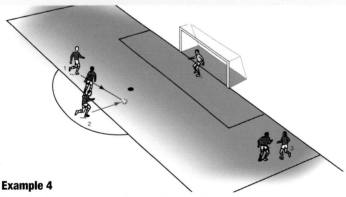

Example 4

Attacker **1** passes to attacker **2** who is onside at the moment the ball is played. The referee, though, has to decide whether there is an offside decision to be made about attacker **3**. He is in an offside position but is a long distance away from active play. But the referee may consider that he is interfering with play by distracting the defender close to him so that the defender doesn't cover attacker **2**. It is a decision that the referee must make quickly.

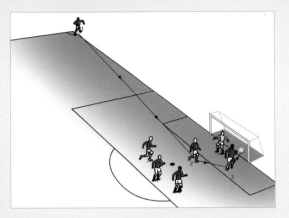

Question 1

Attacker **1** takes a corner kick which travels directly to attacker **2** who shoots, but attacker **3** deflects it into the goal. What is the decision?

Answer

Attacker **2** is not offside direct from the corner kick, but attacker **3** is in an offside position when attacker **2** passes the ball to him. Attacker **3** is nearer the goal line than the ball is, and has only one defender – the goalkeeper – between him and the goal line when the ball is played. Attacker **3** is involved in active play so is offside. The goal is disallowed and an indirect free kick awarded to the defending team.

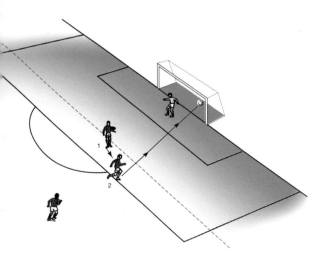

Question 2

Attacker **1** has beaten the defender and passes to attacker **2**, who scores. What is the decision?

Answer

Attacker **2** is not offside when attacker **1** plays the ball, because, at the moment the ball is played, he is not in front of the ball. The goal is awarded.

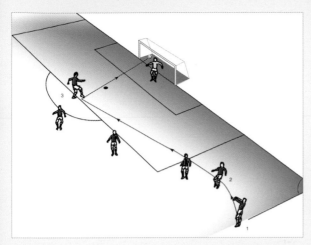

Question 3

Attacker **1** takes a throw-in with the ball going to attacker **2**. He passes it to attacker **3**, who scores. What is the decision?

Answer

Attacker **2** cannot be offside from the throw-in. When the ball is passed to attacker **3**, he is not nearer the goal line than the ball. Attacker **3** is not offside and the goal is awarded.

Question 4

Attacker **1** has dribbled past the defender and shoots. The ball rebounds off the goalpost (red line) or is punched by the goalkeeper (blue line) to attacker **2**, who scores. What is the decision?

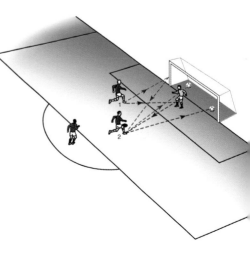

Answer

Attacker **2** is not offside from the rebound, since he is not in front of the ball when it is played by attacker **1**. The referee may choose to award a goal unless he judges that attacker **1** is in an offside position and is interfering with play as attacker **2** shoots.

FREE KICKS

A free kick will be awarded if a player commits an offence (see page 24) or is caught offside (see page 32). The ball must be stationary when a free kick is taken, and the player taking the kick cannot touch the ball for a second time until it has been touched by another player.

There are two types of free kick:

- indirect – from which a goal cannot be scored without the ball touching another player

- direct – from which a goal can be scored direct against the offending side.

Free kick inside own penalty area

All opposing players must be at least 9.15m (10 yds) from the ball. They must also remain outside the penalty area until the ball has been kicked out of the area. If the ball is not kicked directly into play beyond the

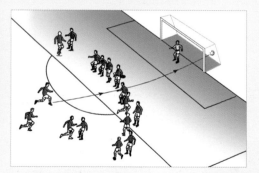

Turn to page 24, to check up on the ten offences for which a direct free kick can be awarded.

In a direct free kick, the taker can strike a shot directly on goal.

In this indirect free kick, player **1** has made a short pass to player **2** who can take a shot on goal.

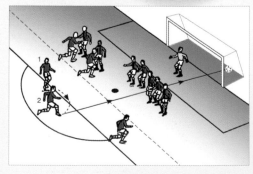

penalty area, the kick is retaken. The goalkeeper must not receive the ball into his hands so that he can kick it into play.

If the free kick is to be taken in the goal area, the ball may be placed at any point within the goal area in which the offence occurred.

Free kick outside own penalty area

The kick must be taken from the place where the infringement happened unless the special circumstances described on page 22 occur. The following rules apply to the kick:

- all players of the offending side must be at least 9.15m (10 yds) from the ball until it is in play

- the ball must be stationary when a free kick is taken, and is in play when it has been kicked and moves

- if, after taking a free kick, the kicker plays the ball a second time before it touches another player, his opponents are awarded an indirect free kick from where the offence occurred.

Defending a close free kick

There is only one exception to the rule about players standing at least 9.15m (10 yds) away from an opposition free kick. It occurs when an indirect free kick is awarded in a side's penalty area less than 9.15m (10 yds) from goal. In this case, the defending players are allowed to stand on their goal line between the posts; otherwise they must keep the regulation distance away from their opponent's free kick.

 Everton players form a wall, under the direction of the referee.

PENALTY KICKS

A penalty kick is awarded for any one of ten offences (see page 24) committed by a defending player in his own penalty area. The penalty kick is taken from the penalty mark, 11m (12 yds) from the mid-point of the goal line.

All players, other than the goalkeeper and the player taking the kick, must be:

- on the field of play

- outside the penalty area

- at least 9.15m (10 yds) from the ball

- behind the penalty mark until the kick has been taken.

The goalkeeper can move along his goal line. He must, though, stay on his goal line between the goalposts until the ball has been kicked by the penalty taker.

The penalty taker must kick the ball forwards, and cannot play the ball a second time until it has touched or been played by another player. A goal can be scored direct from a penalty kick or if the ball touches one of a combination of the goalkeeper, crossbar or goalposts before passing over the line.

Infringements at the penalty kick

For any infringement by the defending side at the taking of the penalty kick:

- if a goal is scored, it is allowed

- if no goal is scored, the kick is retaken.

For any infringement by the attacking team, other than the player taking the kick:

- if a goal is scored, it must be disallowed and the kick retaken

- if no goal is scored, the kick is not retaken.

For any infringement by the penalty taker after the ball is in play, an opponent takes an indirect free kick from the place where the infringement occurred.

Time is always allowed for a penalty kick even at the end of half-time, full-time or the end of a period of extra time.

Jermain Defoe about to strike a penalty. The players waiting outside the box are charging forward in case the shot is parried by the keeper.

PENALTY KICK QUESTIONS

Question 1

Attacker **1** is taking a penalty kick, but before he reaches the ball, attacker **2** runs over the 9.15m (10 yds) penalty arc line. What is the decision?

Answer

Attacker **2** commits an offence. If attacker **1** kicks the ball into goal from the penalty kick, the referee orders the kick to be retaken. If attacker **1** does not put the ball into goal, the kick is not retaken.

Question 2

Attacker **1** takes a penalty kick and the ball strikes the upright and rebounds to attacker **2**; he runs in and scores. What is the decision?

Answer

If attacker **2** has not moved into the penalty area until the kick has been taken, then the goal will stand. There is one possible exception when attacker **1** is in front of attacker **2** as attacker **2** shoots. The referee could judge attacker **1** as involved in active play and give him offside.

Question 3

An attacker takes a penalty kick, but as the ball enters the goal, a defender runs into the penalty area. What is the decision?

Answer

It does not matter if the defender moves before or after the ball is kicked because if it goes into the goal, a goal is scored.

Question 4

Additional time is being allowed for a penalty kick. An attacker takes the kick, which is punched out by the goalkeeper. The same attacker follows up and kicks the ball into goal. What is the decision?

Answer

Additional time is allowed for the penalty kick only. As the goalkeeper saves the kick, the referee signals for full time and no goal is scored.

Frank Lampard of Chelsea and England lines up a penalty shot against Portsmouth in a 2005 Premiership match.

> Once you have decided where the ball is going, don't change your mind while taking the kick.

CONTROLLING THE GAME

The referee and his or her officials are responsible for the smooth running of the match. They have to have a complete knowledge of the rules of the game, be able to keep a clear head under pressure, and must be excellent communicators to ensure that the players know exactly what is going on and who is in charge.

The four officials responsible for the control of a game are:

- an appointed referee, who is in charge
- two assistant referees (one for each touchline)
- a stand-by or fourth official.

REFEREE

Each match is controlled by a referee who has full authority to enforce the Laws of the Game. A referee carries with him:

- two working whistles
- two reliable watches
- a coin
- a notebook and pencil
- a yellow and a red card.

A referee's knowledge

The referee must know the Laws of the Game thoroughly and also how they are applied in a game. Referees and assistant referees should read the rules of the competition that their

OFFICIAL'S CLOTHING

Although sometimes called the men (and women) in black, referees and other officials do not have to wear this colour. The Laws of the Game do not state colours for officials' clothing. Usually, the officials wear kit which marks them out clearly from the players of the two teams.

If you would like to find out how to become a referee, see pages 54 and 55.

match is a part of. They should check particularly for rules which can vary such as the duration of play, extra time and the length of the half-time interval.

The referee's powers

The referee enforces the Laws of the Game and controls the match with the help of the assistant referees and the fourth official. Despite the others' help, the referee is in charge. It is up to him alone to enforce the Laws of the Game. His decision is final and his powers start as he enters the field of play. They continue even if the game is suspended for a short time.

The referee can stop the match in a range of different situations. He can:

- stop, suspend or terminate (end completely) the match, at his discretion, for any infringements of the Laws

- stop, suspend or terminate the match because of outside interference

- stop the match if, in his opinion, a player is seriously injured and should ensure that the injured player is removed from the pitch.

It is up to the referee to restart the match after it has been suspended or stopped.

THE REFEREE'S DUTIES

The referee has a number of different duties. He must ensure that the players' equipment and the ball meet all requirements of the Laws of the Game. The referee also:

- acts as timekeeper and keeps a record of the match

- ensures that no unauthorised persons enter the field of play

- acts on the advice of assistant referees regarding incidents which he has not seen

- allows play to continue until the ball is out of play if a player is, in his opinion, only slightly injured

- ensures that any player bleeding from a wound leaves the field of play. This player can only return after a signal by the referee who must be satisfied that the bleeding has stopped.

AFTER THE GAME

After blowing the final whistle and leaving the pitch, a referee's work is not quite over. He has to provide a match report which includes information on any cautions or dismissals and any other incidents which occurred before, during or after the match.

Punishing offences

The referee makes the decision about whether an offence has occurred and what is the correct penalty or punishment. The referee should:

- punish the more serious offence when a player commits more than one offence at the same time

- take disciplinary action against players guilty of cautionable and sending-off offences. He does not have to do this straight away, but must do it when the ball next goes out of play

- takes action against team officials who do not behave in a responsible manner. He can choose to have them expelled from the pitch and its immediate surroundings, i.e. removed from their team bench.

Playing advantage

The referee can allow play to continue when an offence has occurred.

Known as playing advantage, he may do this when the team offended against gain a benefit such as a good attacking position or a chance of scoring a goal. If the benefit doesn't occur, then he can return and penalise the original offence.

Edgar Davids is shown the yellow card.

ASSISTANT REFEREE

Duties

Two assistant referees are appointed whose duties are to signal:

- when the whole of the ball has passed out of the field of play

- which side is entitled to a corner kick, goal kick or throw-in

- when a player may be penalised for being offside

- when a substitution is requested by one team

- when misconduct or any other incident occurs out of the view of the referee

- whether, at penalty kicks, the goalkeeper has moved forward before the ball has been kicked, and whether the ball has crossed the line.

Assistance

Assistant referees can help and advise a referee about a possible offence when they are closer to the action than the referee. The assistant referees can also help the referee control the match by coming onto the pitch to, for example, separate fighting players.

RELIEVING AN ASSISTANT REFEREE

If an assistant referee unduly interferes or acts in an improper way, the referee has the power to relieve him of his duties and make a report to the appropriate authorities.

Here are the signals made by the assistant referee. He should always carry his flag unfurled so that his signals can be clearly seen.

Throw-in (to the side playing in the direction of the flag)

Goal kick

Flags

The flags used by assistant referees should be of different colours, and are usually provided by the home club. Orange-yellow and bright red have proven to be good colours for flags. The assistant referee should always carry his flag unfurled so that his signals can be clearly seen.

Corner kick

Offside on far side

Offside in a roughly central position

Offside on the assistant referee's side of the field

Substitution

Advising the award of a penalty kick

THE FOURTH OFFICIAL

The fourth official is a qualified referee who is available to replace one of the other officials who may become injured and cannot continue. In addition, he has a range of other possible duties. He can:

- help with substitutions

- supervise behaviour of teams, officials and coaches in the technical areas (see page 11)

- indicate how much time the referee has allowed for stoppages

- report any serious misconduct, such as an off-the ball incident, which may have happened away from the gaze of the other match officials

- indicate to the referee if the wrong player has been cautioned because of mistaken identity.

DIAGONAL SYSTEM OF CONTROL

The assistant referees are positioned to cover a half of the field each and run along their touchline between the corner flag and the halfway line. They aim to keep up with play so they can judge offside decisions and see whether or not the ball has gone out of play.

Referees should strive to keep reasonably close to play at all times. But the play can switch from side to side extremely rapidly. A diagonal system of control (see diagram) helps the three officials work together to cover as much of the pitch as possible and allows them to keep each other in view.

As the referee moves up and down the pitch, he moves in a roughly diagonal fashion. The aim is for the referee and one of his assistants to sandwich the play between them so that the two officials are not in the same area and can see the play from both sides.

The fourth official is in charge of the technical area.

This diagram shows the diagonal system of control. The referee will tend to keep up with play by moving up and down the pitch in a broadly diagonal movement – the darker diagonal zone is just a rough guide. This helps the three officials to cover as much of the pitch as possible.

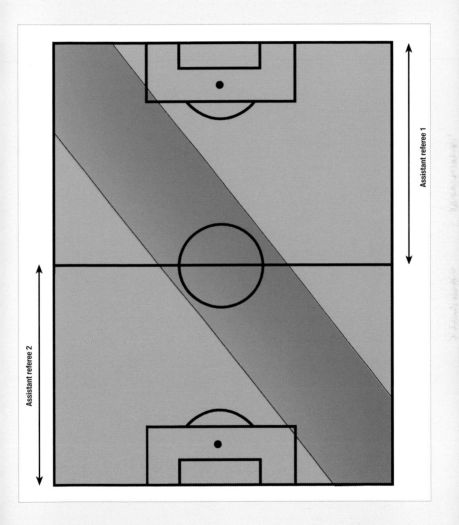

MODIFICATIONS

Football is a sport that can be played by almost anyone – this is part of its global attraction. However, in order for it to be enjoyable, sometimes the Laws of the Game need to be modified.

SCHOOL SOCCER

Some modifications to the game of football can occur providing the principles of the Laws of the Game are kept and that the changes are approved by the national associations. These modifications can be made for schoolchildren up to 16 years of age:

- the size of the field of play
- the size, weight and material of the ball
- the width between the goalposts and the height of the crossbar from the ground
- the duration of the periods of play
- substitutions.

MODIFICATIONS FOR OTHERS

As with schoolchildren, the Laws can be modified for:

- women's soccer
- for veteran's soccer competitions
- for players with disabilities.

As with school soccer, the modifications that can be made relate to the five points listed. Further modifications are allowed only with the consent of the International Board.

Women's soccer has increased in popularity all round the world in the last few decades.

MINI-SOCCER

Mini-soccer is a variation of football for all children under 10 years of age. It is an ideal way to introduce boys and girls to the game as it uses smaller pitches, with scaled down goalposts and fewer players. The emphasis is on fun and inclusion.

Size of pitch

The recommended size of pitch depends on the age of the players.

	Under 10s/9s		Under 8s/7s	
	Metres	**Yards**	**Metres**	**Yards**
Width	Min 27.45 Max 36.6	Min 30 Max 40	Min 18.3 Max 27.45	Min 20 Max 30
Length	Min 45.75 Max 54.9	Min 50 Max 60	Min 27.45 Max 45.75	Min 30 Max 50

On-pitch markings

- Penalty area – length 10 yds (9.15m) x width 18 yds (16.47m)
- Penalty mark – 8 yds (7.32m) from goal line
- Halfway line
- Goal size – distance between posts 12 ft (3.6m) x height 6 ft (1.88m)

Ball size

The ball should be no larger than size 4, and size 3 is recommended for under 8s.

Number of players

Where facilities allow, you should try to use the smaller number of players at the youngest age group, for example 6-a-side for under-9s. Each team must not have a squad greater than double the size of the team.

Number per team, including goalkeeper

Under 10s/9s	6v6 or 7v7
Under 8s/7s	4v4, 5v5, 6v6 or 7v7

Substitutes

Any number of substitutes may be used, and a player who has already been substituted may return to the game as a substitute for another player (these are called 'rolling' substitutions). However, substitutes may only join the game by permission of the referee and during a stoppage in play.

Duration of the game

	Recommended number of minutes each half
Over 6 and under 8s	10 minutes
Over 8 and under 10s	15 minutes

	Maximum playing time per day per player
Over 6 and under 8s	45 minutes
Over 8 and under 10s	60 minutes

THE FOOTBALL ASSOCIATION

The Football Association (FA) was founded in 1863 as the governing body of the game in England. The FA is responsible for all regulatory aspects of the game of football in England.

The FA's activities are many and varied and include:

- promoting the development of the game amongst all ages, backgrounds and abilities

- regulating the game on and off the field of play through the 'Laws of the Game' and the 'Rules of The Association'

- sanctioning all matches, leagues and competitions played in England

- overseeing the running of the disciplinary system which applies to every club, player, official and anyone else involved in the game

- the administration of refereeing throughout the game

- organising many senior men's, youth and women's national competitions (including the FA Challenge Cup) and the participation of England national representative teams in international matches, both friendlies and competitions such as the FIFA World Championships.

The Football Association
25 Soho Square
London
W1D 4FA

Website: www.theFA.com

BECOMING A REFEREE

From playing in the park to the cup final, football needs referees. The following information will give you a clear idea of what training to become and actually being a referee involves.

Who can become a referee?

Anyone with a passion for football. There is a definite benefit in starting young to gain the maximum opportunity to reach the top. However, it's never too late to start if you simply want to continue your enjoyment of the game after your days as a player are over.

Is there a lower age limit?

You may take a course and qualify as a Youth Referee at the age of 14. You will not be able to referee adult football until you reach the age of 16. However, there are plenty of opportunities for refereeing among the younger age groups and in mini-soccer.

Are there opportunities for female match officials?

Female recruits are very welcome to apply. Once qualified you will be able to operate in men's and women's leagues and competitions.

How do I become a referee?

You attend a course organised by your local County Football Association. There is a range of options to suit your particular circumstances, including:

- a number of weekly sessions (usually 6 two-hour lectures)

- a weekend course

- two Saturday or Sunday courses

- a two-part course that allows you to referee with support from a mentor in part two.

Can I get refereeing experience during the course to see if I like it?

The Football Association has designed a course with a practical element built in – the new referee controls three games, under supervision, as part of the course.

Is there a course near to my home?

Yes. Courses are run on a county basis in centres of population. Some are run in schools, colleges and universities. The Armed Forces also organise courses for new referees.

What will it cost me?

There is a small charge for the course, which will be refunded after you have completed your first ten games.

Do I have to pass examinations?

Yes. At the end of the course you will answer a written paper that asks you to decide on the appropriate action to take in a range of circumstances in a game. You will then take an oral examination where the examiner explores your knowledge and understanding of the Laws of the Game.

What else do I need to do in order to qualify?

You will need to pass an eyesight and colour test. You will also have to demonstrate that you can complete a misconduct report correctly.

What happens after I qualify?

You will register as a referee and will then be offered appointments in a league in the area where you live. You will be offered appointments on the days that you make yourself available.

Can I get more training after I qualify?

Yes. You will be offered lots of support all the way through your refereeing career. You will be kept up to date with changes to the Laws of the Game and will receive advice on how to continue to develop your refereeing techniques.

If you are interested in becoming a referee, visit www.theFA.com/TheFA/FALearning.

GLOSSARY

Active play
The area on the field where players are involved in play.

Back pass
A pass by a defender towards the goalkeeper who is not allowed to touch the ball with his hands.

Caution
A form of misconduct for which a player is shown a yellow card.

Centre circle
An area measuring 10 yds (9.15m) diameter in the centre of the field of play at which opponents must stand at the taking of a kick off.

Charges
An illegal challenge usually committed by the shoulder.

Corner
Awarded to the attacking side when a defender last touches the ball (not with his hands) and it goes over his own goal line.

Corner arc
A 1-metre arc at the corner flag at which the ball must be placed when a corner kick is taken.

Crossbar
The horizontal part of the goal which is 8 ft (2.44m) from the ground.

Dangerous play
Play which is deemed to be dangerous, such as a high foot, for which an indirect free kick is awarded.

Defensive wall
Where defenders form a wall, 10 yds (9.15m) from a free kick to block the passage of the ball.

Diagonal system
A system of positioning and movement on the field of play which enables the referee to keep the best view and angle of play.

Direct free kick
A free kick from which a goal can be scored into the opponent's goal.

Disallowed
Where a goal has not been allowed because of an infringement such as offside or an offence has been committed.

Disciplinary action
Where a referee either cautions or send off a player because of his behaviour.

Dismiss
Sending a player from the field of play because they have committed a serious offence such as violent conduct.

Dissent
Usually when a player shows their disagreement with a referee's decision either vocally or by using gestures.

Drop ball
A form of restarting play when the ball is in play and no offence has been committed.

Extra time
An extra period of time, usually 15 minutes each half, played at the end of normal time in Cup matches.

Field of play
The area on which a game of football is played.

FIFA

The international body responsible for football worldwide.

Foul

An illegal challenge committed by a player on an opponent for which a referee awards a free kick.

Fourth official

A referee who is responsible for people in the technical area and who assists the referee and assistants referees control the game.

Formation

A system of play that teams adopt which is designed to overcome the other team.

Friendly

A game played between two teams which is not part of a competition.

Goal

When the whole of the ball passes over the goal line, between the posts and under the crossbar.

Goal area

The area immediately in front of the goals from which goal kicks are taken.

Goal line

The lines at each end of the field of play which extend outwards from the goals.

Golden goal

A form of determining the winner of a game where in extra time the first team to score wins the match.

Handball

A player who deliberately handles the ball using his hand or arm.

IFAB

The International Football Association Board who are responsible for reviewing and making any amendments or additions to the laws of the game.

Impeding

Where a player deliberately blocks the path of an opponent without playing the ball.

Indirect free kick

A free kick which has to be touched or played by another player before a goal can be scored.

Infringement

A term used to indicate when a player commits an offence against an opponent for which a referee will award a free kick.

In play

The time when the ball is in the field of play.

Interference

Being involved either actively with play or with an opponent.

Interfering with play

Actually being involved in play by touching or playing the ball.

Intimidation

A form of threat or when pressure is applied.

Kick-off

A form of starting the match and restarting after a goal has been scored.

Laws of the Game

The seventeen laws of the game which determine how play and players should progress.

FOOTBALL CHRONOLOGY

Football has come a long way since it all began back in 1848. Since then, many important milestones have been reached, from the introduction of referees to the first million-pound player. Here are some of the major dates in the history of the game.

1848 First set of football rules drawn up at Cambridge University.

1863 The Football Association formed in England.

1869 Goal kicks added to rules.

1871 Football's oldest surviving competition, the FA Cup is created.

1872 First football international – a 0–0 draw between England and Scotland.

1872 Corner kicks introduced for the first time.

1873 Scottish and Welsh FAs formed.

1874 Shinpads invented and used by Samuel Widdowson of Nottingham Forest.

1882 Throw-ins now had to be two-handed.

1882 Foundation of the International Football Association Board.

1889 The Netherlands FA was formed – the oldest outside of Britain. It was followed rapidly by football associations in Denmark, Belgium, Switzerland, Sweden, Italy, Germany, Uruguay and Spain.

1890 Goal nets invented by J A Brodie of Liverpool.

1891 Penalty kicks introduced.

1891 Referees put in charge of football matches.

1902 First major footballing disaster when terracing collapsed at Ibrox Park.

1904 Foundation of Fédération Internationale de Football Association (FIFA).

1905 Alf Common becomes world's first £1,000 or equivalent transfer, moving from Sunderland to Middlesbrough.

1905 First South American international match – Uruguay v Argentina.

1908 Football features at the Olympics for the first time.

1910 The first Copa America competition occurs. It features just three teams: Argentina, Chile and Uruquay.

1912 Goalkeepers now only allowed to handle ball in their own penalty area.

1913 'Ten yards' rule at free kicks introduced and applied to corners the following year.

1918 French FA formed.

1925 Offside rule altered from three opposition players nearer the goal line to two.

1930 First World Cup Finals in Uruguay.

1954 Union of European Football Associations (UEFA) founded.

1955 First season of the European Champion Clubs Cup.

1960 Final of the first European Championship.

1966 England win the World Cup.

1970 Brazil win the World Cup for the third time and are given the trophy – the Jules Rimet trophy – to keep. A new trophy – the FIFA World Cup Trophy – is now presented to the World Cup winners.

1979 Trevor Francis becomes the first million-pound player when he moves from Birmingham to Nottingham Forest.

1991 Change to offside law when offside is level with second opponent.

1992 Formation of Premier League.

1992 The European Cup becomes the UEFA Champions League.

1997 Laws of the Game revised into current modern format.

2004 Offence for players to remove shirt as part of goal scoring celebration.

INDEX

assistant referees 44, 45, 46, 48–49
  diagonal system 50, 51
  offside 32, 33, 34

backpass rule 31
ball 6, 7
Beckham, David 17
bench 11, 16, 17
bleeding injury 46
boots 6
boundary lines 8

Campbell, Sol 7
captains 14, 15, 19
caution 24, 26, 28, 46, 50
centre circle 9, 10
children 7, 52, 53
Chopra, Michael 15
clothing 4, 26, 44
coaches 11, 50
corner 9, 13, 23
corner flag 12, 13, 20, 50
corner kick 9, 18, 22
  assistant referee 48, 49
  corner flagposts 13
  misconduct 28
  offside 33, 35, 36
crossbar 9, 12, 17, 20, 40, 52
cup competitions 16

dangerous play 24, 25
Davids, Edgar 27, 46
deflection 36
Defoe, Jermain 41
diagonal system 50
disabilities 52
dismissal 24, 46
dissent 28
dribbling 37
Drogba, Didier 31
dropped ball 16, 22
Dudek, Jerzy 18
dugout 11

equipment 4–7, 46

Euro 2000 19
extra time 15, 19, 40, 45

FIFA 14
flags 32, 48, 49
footwear 4, 6
foul play 28
fourth official 44, 45, 50
free kick 18, 38–39
  corner kick 22
  goal kick 22
  goalkeeper 31
  handball 17
  kick-off 14
  misconduct 28
  offences 24, 25, 26
  offside 36
  penalty area 10
  penalty kicks 40
  suspension of play 16
  throw-in 21
full-time 40, 43

Gerrard, Steven 7
gloves 4
goal 4, 12, 18, 53
  corner kick 22
  free kicks 38
  kick-off 14
  offside 36
  penalty kicks 40, 43
  scoring 17, 21
goal area 9, 10, 12–13
  dropped ball 22
  free kick 39
  goal kick 22
goal kick 9, 18, 22, 23
  assistant referee 48
  goal area 12
  offside 33, 35
  penalty area 10
  suspension of play 16
goal line 8, 9
  ball out of play 20
  corner flagposts 13
  corner kick 22
  free kick 39

goal kick 22
offside 32, 34, 36
penalty kick 40
penalty mark 11
scoring 17
goalkeeper 4, 12, 31
  assistant referee 48
  free kicks 39
  goal 12
  goal kick 22
  misconduct 28
  modifications 53
  offences 24, 25
  offside 36, 37
  penalties 19
  penalty area 10, 11
  penalty kick 40, 41, 43
  throw-in 21
goalposts 9, 12
  ball out of play 20
  free kick 39
  modifications 52, 53
  offside 37
  penalty kick 40
  scoring 17
Golden Goal 19

half-time 14, 40, 45
halfway line 8, 9, 13, 50, 53
handling the ball 17, 24, 25, 26, 28, 31
Hughes, Michael 29

impeding 24, 27
infringements 14, 16, 32, 33, 39, 40, 45
injury 15, 16, 45, 46, 50
International Board 52
international matches 8, 9

kick-off 9, 10, 14
Kirkland, Chris 23
kit 5, 6

Lampard, Frank 2, 5, 43
Laws of the Game 8, 24, 44, 45, 46, 52
leagues 4, 16

managers 11
markings 8, 9, 53
match report 46
mini-soccer 53
misconduct 28–29, 48, 50
Mori, Damien 14

nets 12
Neville, Phil 21
numbers 4

obstruction 24, 27
off-the ball incidents 50
offences 24–31
  assistant referee 48
  free kicks 38, 39
  goal kick 22
  goalkeepers 31
  offside 32, 33
  penalty area 10
  penalty kicks 40, 43
  referee 46
offensive language 28
officials 13, 44–51
offside 32–37
  assistant referee 48, 49, 50
  free kicks 38
  halfway line 9
  throw-in 20
onside 33
own goal 22

Parker, Scott 15
penalty 6, 9, 10, 11, 17, 19, 21
penalty area 9, 10
  free kicks 18, 38, 39
  goal kick 22
  goalkeepers 31
  handball 17
  misconduct 28
  modifications 53
  offences 24, 25
  offside 34
  penalty kicks 40, 43
penalty kick 2, 19, 21, 40–43
  assistant referee 48, 49
  misconduct 28

offences 24
time added on 15
penalty mark 9, 11, 40, 53
penalty shootouts 19
pitch 7, 8, 9, 52, 53
playing advantage 46
Premier League 7
Premiership 2, 27, 43

rebound 37, 43
red card 17, 28, 29, 44
referee 44–51
assistant referee 48
ball change 7
clothing 4
diagonal system 50
extra time 15
fourth official 50
free kicks 39
goalkeepers 31
hand ball 26
kick-off 14
kit 5
misconduct 28, 29
modifications 53
offences 24, 25
offside 32, 33, 35, 37
penalty kicks 43
penalty shootouts 19
substitutions 16
suspension of play 16
time added on 15
Ricardo 19
Robinson, Paul 31

Savage, Robbie 29
school soccer 52
scoring 17, 19, 21
sending off 5, 17, 24, 29, 46
Shearer, Alan 15
Sheringham, Teddy 27
Shevchenco, Andriy 18
shinguards 4, 5
six-a-side 53
six-second rule 25, 31
spectacles 4
spitting 24, 28

squad 53
stoppage time 50
strip 4
studs 6
substitution 16
assistant referee 48, 49
fourth official 50
modifications 52, 53
time added on 15
suspension of play 16, 22

tackle 24, 26
tactics 15, 28
teams 4
technical area 11, 29, 50
throw-in 8, 20, 21
assistant referee 48
goalkeeper 31
offences 25
offside 33, 35, 37
suspension of play 16
time wasting 15
timekeeper 46
touchline 8, 9
assistant referees 44, 50
ball out of play 20
corner flagposts 13
technical area 11
throw-in 20, 21
training 7

UEFA Champions League 18

wall 39
women's soccer 52

yellow card 28, 29, 44

Zidane, Zinedine 33